Brain-Healing First Aid

How to Recover My Brain's Abilities During Addiction Treatment

(Version 3)

Authors:
Hamed Ekhtiari, MD, PhD
Tara Rezapour, PhD
Brad Collins, MHR, LADC
Martin Paulus, MD

Brain-Healing First Aid

How to Recover My Brain's Abilities During Addiction Treatment

Authors
Hamed Ekhtiari, MD, PhD
Tara Rezapour, PhD
Brad Collins, MHR, LADC
Martin Paulus, MD
This edition is published in 2020

More Details: Ekhtiari H., Rezapour T., Aupperle R., Paulus M. (2017). Neuroscience-informed psychoeducation for addiction medicine: A neurocognitive perspective. Progress in Brain Research. 235; 239-264

ISBN-13: 978-1-7347408-4-4

Illustrators: Naeem Tadayon, Samira Mokhtari
Graphic Designer: Mohsen Farhadi

The material of this book is not intended to replace the services of your physician, therapist, or caregiver. Since the recovery process for each person is unique, you should consult with your own physician or therapist to evaluate the symptoms you may have, or to receive suggestions for appropriate interventions.

This book is written based on the latest findings in cognitive neuroscience and authors have tried their best to make it as accurate and up to date as possible. However, it may contain errors, oversights, or materials that is out of date at the time you read it. The authors and publisher disclaim any legal responsibility or liability for errors, oversights, and out-of-date materials, or the reader's application of the information or advice contained in this book.

Copyright © 2020 by H. Ekhtiari. All rights reserved. This book may not be reproduced, in whole or in part, including illustrations, in any form (beyond that copyright permitted by Sections 107 and 108 of the U.S. Copyright Law and except by reviewers for the public press), without written permission from the publishers.

Printed in the United States of America

Preface

The brain disease of addiction (and long-term substance use) results in many symptoms. Much of the time, if left untreated, these diminished brain functions can progress into a number of inevitably debilitating conditions. Our brain is the control center for essentially every function needed to perform daily tasks and the control center for our body and all its organs. We often take this truth (and our brain health) for granted. Even after years of neglect and abuse, our brain and the numerous functions previously available to us (many we may have lost in addiction) can be restored.

Brain Awareness Recovery Initiative (BARI) is a collaborative project created to produce and distribute educational materials designed to help the person in early addiction recovery identify areas of need for intervention and track progress achieved in brain function restoration. An important goal may be to build a solid foundation in all facets of recovery. BARI provides a series of tools, few of many resources a person challenged by addiction needs to sustain long-term recovery.

"Brain-Healing First Aid: How to Recover my Brain's Abilities during Addition Treatment" and our three poster series, as our first productions in the BARI, can offer identification of problem areas, new insight, helpful suggestions, and specific brain exercises for healing to help you put more "tools in your toolbox" to assist in creating a sustainable recovery plan. Not every area and/or suggestion will fit everyone. We have used numerous resources to come up with common brain function deficits experienced by a majority of people negatively affected by substance use and drug addiction.

We hope you find our posters and the contents of "Brain Healing First Aid" to be useful "go-to" resources in your recovery. If you have any questions, feedback or suggestions, we would love to hear from you. Please send you emails to bari.braingym@gmail.com or post on our webpage: http://www.laureateinstitute.org/bari-posters.html In the meantime, we wish you the best on your journey in recovery.

Tips on How to Use this Book

This is our companion book to our Brain Awareness Recovery Initiative (BARI) posters. Poster 1 (of our 3 BARI posters) identifies 10 main areas of brain functions compromised in substance abuse and addiction. Poster 2 offers general suggestions about new attitudes and healthier habits you can adopt to lay a strong foundation for your brain-healing and recovery. Poster three outlines detailed brain exercises, specific to the identified areas of the brain which are likely to need function restoration or improvement. All of the poster strategies are reiterated in our companion book in to four sessions / parts. Using "Brain Healing First-Aid…" to complement the posters and document tasks you have completed and writing down the results can help you build a strong habit association with brain exercises and sustained recovery. Also, tracking your brain-healing progress can create optimism and confidence for you to be able to perform tasks, regulate emotions and drug craving, over which you may have lost control in addiction.

This book will not provide you everything that you need during the process of brain recovery but it can offer you with a very good starting point.

Use this book to chronicle your progress and reward yourself, in different, healthy ways for a job well done. You are worth your own effort to heal!

Table of contents

10 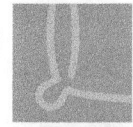 **Part I**
Be more attentive and remember better

30  **Part II**
Be more calm and sleep better

58  **Part III**
Be more explorer and decide better

80 **Part IV**
Be more social and feel better

Part I

Be more attentive and remember better

Have you ever experienced spending time searching for your glasses while you are wearing them? Or are you afraid of roach as much as you jump out of your skin if you see anything brown? Welcome to the first part!

Attention   Memory

Attention

I often experience that environmental triggers can produce an inability in me to control my desire to use my drug of preference, even when I do not want to use because using is all I can think about. When this happens, I have very little ability to shift my focus to anything else. Even carrying-on a conversation with someone is very difficult when I am locked-on to thinking about using. Multi-tasking of any kind is nearly impossible when I am pulled into thinking about drug use when driven by environmental cues.

What are the other aspects of "Attention Deficits" you've experienced in your life? List and discuss them in writing here:

....

....

....

Have you ever:
- Found it difficult to concentrate on activities like reading books or listening to an ongoing conversation? ☐ Yes ☐ No
- Found it impossible to focus on task you are doing with TV is on background or other people are talking around you? ☐ Yes ☐ No
- Found it confusing when you try to do two things at the same time (for example washing the dishes and talking on the phone)? ☐ Yes ☐ No
- Found it very difficult to stay focused more than 20 minutes on one task (for example attending to a lecture)? ☐ Yes ☐ No
- Found it very hard to react quickly to something happens unexpectedly (for example a fast moving car coming straight at you)? ☐ Yes ☐ No

The questions above are some examples of situations that you need to use your attention. So, the more "Yes" responses, the more you need to care about your attention.

....

....

....

....

....

1. Scan the below image with your eyes and try to find as many target pictures (three-leaf clovers) without marking anything on the paper. Write the total number that you find.

2. For 5 minutes, try to find as many of the hidden items as you can and mark them.

3. Consider the different lines of shapes below. Whenever you find the target pattern (five and three dot dices) in a row, count them.

How many can you find in 2 minutes? ....

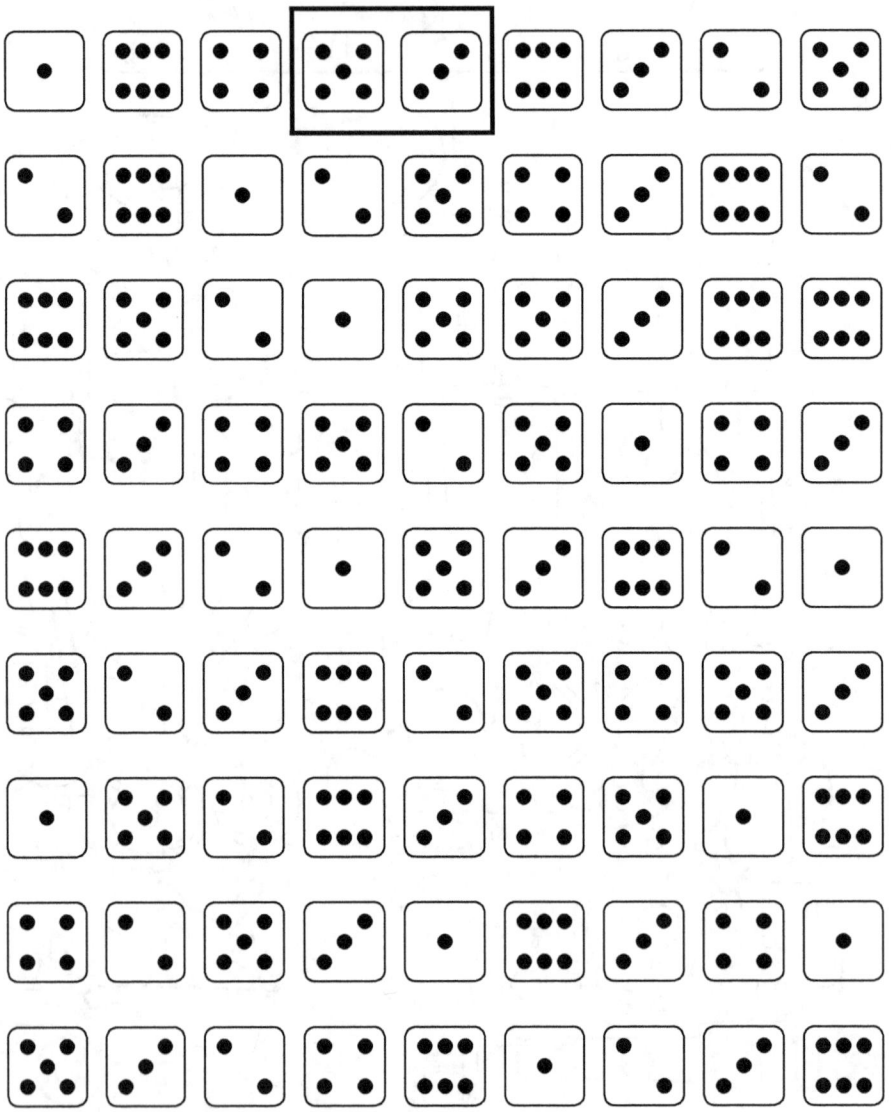

4. Here you are presented with a list of numbers written with different colors (e.g., "20"). You should alternate between reporting whether the number is smaller or bigger than "10" (S or B) and reporting whether the number is odd or even (O or E). The first few are done for you as an example.

9	25	16	21	6	17	12	27	31	4
SO	BO								
19	14	3	16	8	19	2	22	37	12
8	18	23	29	17	24	4	1	22	17
12	21	14	5	12	1	17	26	3	26
21	11	7	2	17	15	9	12	13	1
13	5	12	6	11	8	15	3	8	14
22	14	8	19	1	11	7	16	2	19
7	12	11	15	2	21	11	16	6	3

Practice

Attention

- **Do Word Exercises:** Practice reverse spelling during daily conversation and spell the words you hear backward in your mind. Ex: Apple could be elppa in your "Brain language"

- **Be Your "Present-Moment" Attention Coach:** You can practice controlling your attention and lessen your brain's tendency to wander during important tasks. Intentional, gentle and internal messages such as "focus on the task at hand" or "come back to the present moment" can become a habit to bring you back into focus.

- **Train Your Brain to be Flexible:** Try to shift between two or more brain tasks as a daily exercise. Ex: Practice a Sudoku puzzle for 10 min and then shift to solving a crossword for 10 min and then return to the Sudoku again.

Identify and describe other recovery activities you may be aware of or already be using you believe are useful.

....
....
....
....
....
....
....

5. Write down the word "Square" in the rectangle-shaped boxes and the word "Rectangle" in the square-shaped boxes. Do them in order as quickly as possible.

Memory

I believe my memory has been negatively affected by my drug use. I seem to experience "involuntary" memories related to my using such as when I pass by or think about places where I would use. I am experiencing lapses in short-term memory, forgetting things as recent as what I had for lunch or if I returned a phone call. I feel like this may cause others to lose trust in me.

What are the other aspects of "Memory Deficits" you've experienced in your life? List and discuss them in writing here:

....
....

Have you ever:

- Found that your memory doesn't work as well as it used to be?
  ☐ Yes ☐ No
- Found it difficult to remember the information you have learned recently (for example new phone numbers, new names, new addresses)?
  ☐ Yes ☐ No
- Forgotten the food recipes you always cooked? ☐ Yes ☐ No
- Forgotten the routes that you always took them to home? ☐ Yes ☐ No
- Found it difficult to memorize shopping list or names of familiar people?
  ☐ Yes ☐ No

The questions above are some examples of situations that you need to use your memory. So, the more "Yes" responses, the more you need to care about your memory.

....
....
....

6. Look at the below pictures for 25 seconds and then turn to the next page.

Without returning to the previous page, try to recall as many pictures as you can.

....
....
....
....
....
....
....

7. Look at the below pictures for 25 seconds and then turn to the next page.

Without returning to the previous page, try to find all changes in this picture compared to the previous one.

8. Look at the below picture for 20 seconds and then turn to the next page.

9. Without turning to the previous page answer these questions:

A. How many people were in the picture?

a. 4 people ☐
b. 5 people ☐
c. 6 people ☐

B. Which animal you saw in the picture?

a. Cat ☐
b. Dog ☐
c. Rabbit ☐

C. Which one was on the floor?

a. Dish ☐
b. Toy ☐
c. Book ☐

D. What were children eating?

a. Fruit ☐
b. Ice-cream ☐
c. Tea ☐

10. Without returning to the previous page, try to recall as many pictures as you can from the first memory exercise.

....
....
....
....
....

Practice

Memory

- **Journal in Your Brain Book:** Document important events that influenced your day every night. You can visualize and observe the events of your day as if watching a play.

- **Play "Memory Games":** Prepare a list of information such as a grocery list or a word list every day and try to memorize it throughout the day. Commit a snapshot of the list to memory for ready-access, so new words will be available when you need them.

- **Reduce "Brain Clutter":** Try to reduce the load of information taking up your brain-space by economizing strands into smaller, associated "chunks". Ex: Instead of remembering 140593251, simplify to 140-593-251. Any other innovative ways to organize and chunk information will help your memory.

Identify and describe other recovery activities you may be aware of or already be using you believe are useful.

....
....
....
....
....
....

Try to write down the activities you did yesterday? Start from the morning and go through the whole day	
06:00 a.m.	04:00 p.m. ....
07:00 a.m.	05:00 p.m. ....
08:00 a.m.	06:00 p.m. ....
09:00 a.m.	07:00 p.m. ....
10:00 a.m.	08:00 p.m. ....
11:00 a.m.	09:00 p.m. ....
12:00 p.m.	10:00 p.m. ....
01:00 p.m.	11:00 p.m. ....
02:00 p.m.	12:00 a.m. ....
03:00 p.m.	01:00 a.m. ....

Few Suggestions
Be more mentally active

- **Honor** the fact that your brain needs exercise along with your body to be able to regain its fully-integrated functions.
- **Be willing** to do brain exercises which are systematically designed for improvement of brain functions.
- **Progress gradually** into difficult and challenging levels of brain exercise, much like you might increase the weights in gym exercises. Follow the recommendations of a counselor, recovery coach or other helping professional in regard to the type and level of mental exercises you practice.

Identify and describe other recovery activities you may be aware of or already be using you believe are useful.

....
....
....
....
....

11. Among the hands below, find the right hands and the left hands.

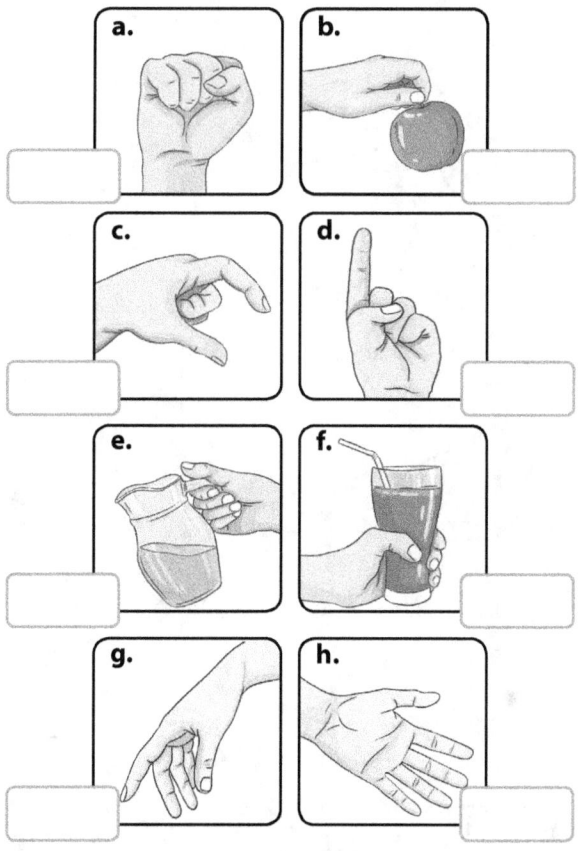

Few Suggestions
Be a healthy foodie

- **Include** more fruit especially berries and dark green leafy vegetables in your diet. Their natural antioxidants and vitamins will help your brain to recover injured and inflamed areas.

- **Eats lots** of oily fish (salmon and tuna) and eggs. Their micronutrients will provide your brain with materials to restore its disturbed structures.

- **Reduce** salt intake and make intentional efforts to lower Cholesterol.

Identify and describe other recovery activities you may be aware of or already be using you believe are useful.

....
....
....
....
....
....

You have done the first session and learned about "Attention" and "Memory". Now, mark the scales below:

Your mood:

0   1   2   3   4   5   6   7   8   9   10

Level of Achievement:

0   1   2   3   4   5   6   7   8   9   10

Date: ....   Time: ....   Duration: ....

Number of incorrect answers: ....

Main weak points: ....
....
....

Conclusion: ....
....
....

Part II
Be more calm and sleep better

Have you experienced overeating when you are stressed? Or do you have problem falling asleep at night and feel dead-tired during day? Or get anxious without any reason?
Welcome to the second part!

| Brain Body Connection | Feeling Bad | Sleep and Arousal |

Feeling Bad

I often experience negative feelings like a dramatic sense of guilt, becoming stuck in self-debasement, and a profound fear of abandonment. Experiencing these feelings around my drug use creates a great deal of anxiety, even confuses and angers me. Certain words and sounds can be distressing, causing me to feel intensified anxiety and stress. These negative feelings result in an intense DRUG CRAVING in me. Despite evidence from experience to the contrary, I can still find myself believing that using drugs is the only solution to help me relax and feel better.

What are the other aspects of "Feeling Bad Deficits" you've experienced in your life? List and discuss them in writing here:

....
....
....

Have you ever:

- Felt anxious without any certain reason? ☐ Yes ☐ No
- Felt afraid without any specific reason or got stressed about little things? ☐ Yes ☐ No
- Found it difficult to manage and control your stress? ☐ Yes ☐ No
- Gotten easily angered or annoyed due to an unimportant word? ☐ Yes ☐ No
- Gotten upset after watching a dramatic movie and mentally engaged with the movie during the whole day? ☐ Yes ☐ No

The questions above are some examples of situations that you need to control your negative emotions. So, the more "Yes" responses, the more you need to care about your negative emotions.

....
....
....
....
....
....

1. Try to find and circle all the neutral words as fast as you can.

Sad
War
Attack
Worried
Cheater
Tea
Alone   Kitchen
Fork
Accident
Anger
Table
Injury
Gun
Bird   Note   Failure
Shout
Grief   Fire
Net
Park   Window
Divorce
Pain   Sick   Hospital
Pen   Pizza

2. Try to say the ink color of the words below, as fast as you can, while ignoring the meaning of the word.

Pipe	Hit	Smack	Blow	Crack
Meth	Rush	Chore	Alcohol	Smack
Drug	Bar	Hash	Puff	Dealer
Chore	Pipe	Alcohol	Crack	Smack
Dealer	Blow	Bar	Puff	Meth
Crack	Hash	Alcohol	Rush	Hit
Chore	Smack	Dealer	Crack	Pipe
Blow	Meth	Chore	Pipe	Dealer
Bar	Rush	Drug	Smack	Alcohol
Hash	Alcohol	Dealer	Hit	Meth
Hit	Crack	Pipe	Puff	Blow

Practice
Feeling Bad

- **Use Positive Language:** Replace negative words with positive ones. Use positive affirmations such as: "Look how far I have come" as opposed to: "I am not progressing fast enough."

- **Live in Gratitude:** Consistently acknowledge things for which you are grateful. To your recovery friends, to your family, to yourself and to your spiritual life. Make a list of areas and things in your life for which you are grateful.

- **Volunteer for Charity Work and Express Your Spiritual Generosity:** Help other people even if it seems small. Volunteering or charity work is a great opportunity to be of service to others.

Identify and describe other recovery activities you may be aware of or already be using you believe are useful.

....

....

....

Try to write down a list of positive phrases that you would feel calm and happy by you repeat them. See the examples below:

1. *I am sure that everything will go well.*
2. *Today is a great day.*
3. ....

Brain-Body Connection

I do not feel like I am in touch with my bodily senses anymore. When I am stressed, craving, depressed or anxious I do not feel like my mind and body communicate; therefore, I am not aware what my body may need at certain times, such as when I need to hydrate, when I am hungry, or fatigued. It's like my mind and body are completely out of touch with each other. My emotions often present themselves through bodily sensations, so when I don't pay attention to my "gut level senses", the result is an inability to control these emotions.

What are the other aspects of "Brain-Body Connection Deficits" you've experienced in your life? List and discuss them in writing here:

....
....
....

Can you write about an event that has happened recently and made you feel upset and annoyed? Try to write about the physical and mental changes that you experienced at that time.

....
....
....
....
....
....
....
....
....
....
....
....
....
....
....

3. Look at the picture below and try to describe both the physical sensations and the emotions you think the person in this picture might be experiencing.

4. Try to answer the below questions.

■ How many times your heart beats in one minute? Try to estimate it using your watch without touching your pulse: .... beats per minute

Now try to measure it and see how much it differs with your estimation.

> To check your pulse at your wrist, place two fingers between the bone and the tendon over your radial artery — which is located on the thumb side of your wrist. When you feel your pulse, count the number of beats in 60 seconds. Manage your attention to not get distracted to other things around you and miss a pulse.

The result of your measurement: .... beats per minute.

■ Let's do the same with our breathing rate. How many breaths do you take in one minute? Try to guess ....

Now, try to focus on your breathing and count it in one minute and see how much it differs with your earlier estimation.

The result of your measurement: .... per minute

■ What do you feel in your stomach at the moment?

....

....

....

....

....

....

....

5. Can you imagine the below situations and write about the emotion and internal state you may experience in each situation. See the example below.

Situation	Emotion	Internal Sensations
At my friend's birthday party, I gave her a present that she already had and obviously couldn't use.	Embarrassed, anxious, regretful	Hot Ears, red face and tightened throat
Losing your wallet		
Being surprised by your friends for your birthday		
Standing near the scene of the accident		

6. Link the rose and leaf consecutively (rose to leaf to rose and so on), without raising your pencil. Note that you cannot pass through each rose and leaf more than onces. The first few are done as an example. Count your breath.

Number of breaths: ....

Practice
Brain-Body Connection

- **Practice Body-Presence:** Focus on your body while you are exercising, practicing yoga, sitting in meditation, etc. instead of listening to the music. Experience the communication created between your brain and body and feelings associated with it.

- **Observe Your Heart Rate:** Check your pulse several times during different activities throughout the day. Tune-in to the message your pulse and heart rate will offer at various conditions. Try different ways to check your pulse. Even try to feel your heart beat without touching your external body. Can you sense it?

- **Practice Mindfulness:** Observe your environment and your body with curiosity and pay attention to sounds around you as if it is your first time to experience them.

Identify and describe other recovery activities you may be aware of or already be using you believe are useful.

....
....
....

The exercise below is a sample of a mindfulness exercise that you can do everyday.

1. Find a quite and comfortable place to sit. You can sit on the floor or on a chair or sofa. The important thing is that you should sit up straight.

2. Try to focus on your muscles. Do you feel any tension or pain in your muscle? You can keep your eyes closed or half open. Keeping your eyes closed can help to be more focused. Try to listen to the sounds inside your body (e.g., heartbeat, breath).

3. Try to focus on your breath, the inhale and exhale. Try not to change the rhythm. If you get distracted by other things around, try to return your attention and focus on breathing.

By repeating these exercises and the other similar ones, you can see your progress in controlling your attention.

....
....
....
....
....
....
....

Arousal and Sleep

I have a difficult time falling asleep and staying asleep. I wake-up startled and anxious. I can feel my heart beat too loudly, remain anxious, excitable and easily aroused. I find it very hard to become calm once I am experiencing these states. In contrast, sometimes I feel drowsy and sleepy when I believe I should be alert during work. My body, mental state, and emotional being feel heavy and I often find physical movement and motivation to move very challenging.

What are the other aspects of "Arousal and Sleep Deficits" you've experienced in your life? List and discuss them in writing here:

Have you ever tried to find the reason(s) that may disturb your night sleep? For example, eating heavy dinner, stressful events, etc. Try to write down a list of reasons that may affect your night sleep.

7. Are you a good sleeper? Check your sleep quality and quantity.

#	Question	Yes	No
1	Do you often have problem getting enough sleep at night?		
2	Do you often have difficulty falling asleep despite being tired at night?		
3	Do you often find it difficult to stay awake the whole day without taking a nap?		
4	Do you wake up frequently during the night?		
5	Do you often find it difficult to wake up in the morning?		
6	Do you often have nightmares?		
7	Do you often wake up in the middle of the night and have difficulties getting back to sleep?		
8	Do you often sleep less than 6 hours?		
9	Do you often fall asleep during the day, while you are doing your regular daily activities (e.g. reading books)?		
10	Is your sleep/wake time inconsistent?		
11	Do you often feel tired and have no energy in the morning?		
12	Do you have excessive daytime sleepiness?		
13	Do you often experience sleep-walk?		
14	Do you always think that you need more sleep?		
	Total	/14	/14

The questions above are some examples of the sleep problems that you may experience due to various reasons. The more "Yes" responses, the more you need to care about your sleep hygiene.

8. Scan the images below and try to find and count the left-pointing arrows without marking them. Do them in order without skipping around.

Total: ....

Practice

Arousal and Sleep

- **Create a Sleep Haven:** Prepare your bedroom for a relaxing and soothing sleep by making it dark and quiet. Turn your electronic devices to silent and offer yourself comforting supports, such as an ideal pillow.

- **Pamper Yourself Occasionally:** Utilize spa activities such as massage, sauna, hot tub, manicure, pedicure, etc. whenever possible. You can even use your home bathtub as your personal spa.

- **Enjoy the Benefits of Warmth/Heat:** Take a warm shower to ease tension in your muscles. Set your home water on a therapeutic temperature to relax your joints and muscles.

Identify and describe other recovery activities you may be aware of or already be using you believe are useful.

....
....
....

Did you know that people often categorized in two groups of "Morningness" or "Eveningness"?

■ Morningness people are those people who easily wake up early at the morning and their peak performance tends to be during morning. This group of people spend the evening watching tv or doing activities that doesn't take a lot of mental energy to be concentrated.

■ Eveningness people are those people who wake up late at the morning since they stay up late doing tasks that require concentration. This group of people doesn't have a high level of performance during mornings.

What is your type? Are you a morningness or eveningness person?

....
....
....
....
....
....
....
....

Few Suggestions

Be calm and relaxed

- **Not unlike** other bodily injuries, your brain needs sufficient time to become peaceful and calm to experience healing.

- **Stress** is your brain's worst enemy and exposure to heightened stress hampers the recovery process.

- **Avoid** when possible, people, places, events and other things that tend to raise your stress level. You can start to gradually and slowly expose yourself to the normal life stressors after the first few months of recovery under supervision of your counsellors and therapists.

Identify and describe other recovery activities you may be aware of or already be using you believe are useful.

....
....
....
....
....
....
....

9. Color the mandala below. Try to focus on colors as you use them.

Few Suggestions
Be in tune with your emotions

- **Learn and practice** problem-solving strategies in order to deal with daily life problems.
- **Gain** skills to practice emotional awareness in order to identify and separate various emotional states and feelings.
- **Attend** leisure and recreation activities that can soothe and restore your brain.

Identify and describe other recovery activities you may be aware of or already be using you believe are useful.

....
....
....
....
....
....
....
....

Try to prepare a list of joyful activities. These activities could be as simple as drinking a cup of coffee.

....
....
....
....
....
....
....
....
....
....

Brain Healing First Aid: Part II

Few Suggestions
Be a healthy sleeper

- **Your brain** needs sufficient (but not too much) sleep at night and periods of daytime rest to recharge.

- **Turn** your bedroom into a sleep haven; calm and dark with proper temperature. This will help your brain to take advantage of sleep as much as possible for its recovery.

- **Commit** to and maintain a regular, healthy and helpful sleep schedule. Fixed daily schedule for sleep will help your brain to be rested and accessible when you need it.

Identify and describe other recovery activities you may be aware of or already be using you believe are useful.

....

....

....

Try to record the sleeping and waking times during this week.

Mon	Tue	Wed	Thur	Fri	Sat	Sun
:	:	:	:	:	:	:

You have done the second session and learned about "Feeling bad", "Brain-Body connection" and "Arousal/sleep" Now, mark the scales below:

Your mood:

0 1 2 3 4 5 6 7 8 9 10

Level of Achievement:

0 1 2 3 4 5 6 7 8 9 10

Date: .... Time: .... Duration: ....

Number of incorrect answers: ....

Main weak points: ....

....

....

Conclusion: ....

....

....

Part III

Be more explorer and decide better

Have you ever experienced difficulties with making a simple decision or regretting your choices you have made? Or have you recently noticed that you become slowly in your actions even while you are talking. Finding the proper words during conversation is not easy as pie anymore.
Welcome to third part!

| Decision and Control | Movement and Speech |

Decisions & Control

I can make a decision to refrain from using but many times, I am unable to follow-through with my decision. I feel powerless over my ability to not use, even when I don't want to, especially if I have recently used. Once I am in the presence of and actually see my drug of preference, I lose control. I cannot successfully choose to not use, as if a powerful force takes over and I am at the mercy of craving my drug, using despite my resolve not to. When I am craving, I feel emotionally unstable, my mood changes quickly from happy-to-sad, angry-to-rage, without much stimulus to incite the change. It just happens, without my permission.

What are the other aspects of "Decisions & Control Deficits" you've experienced in your life? List and discuss them in writing here:

....
....
....
....
....

Have you ever:

- Found it difficult to control yourself to not jump into an ongoing conversation while other people are talking? ☐ Yes ☐ No
- Talked improperly in a group of friends or colleagues? ☐ Yes ☐ No
- Made a decision that you regretted later? ☐ Yes ☐ No
- Acted impulsively and without prior thought? ☐ Yes ☐ No
- Preferred a small but immediate reward rather than a bigger but the delayed one? ☐ Yes ☐ No

The questions above are some examples of situations that you need to use your control and decision making. So, the more "Yes" responses, the more you need to care about these functions.

....
....
....
....
....
....
....
....

1. Draw the arrows that match the direction of the dark gray fish. For the light gray fish, draw the arrow in the opposite direction. See the examples below and finish the rest as quickly as you can. Do them in order without skipping around.

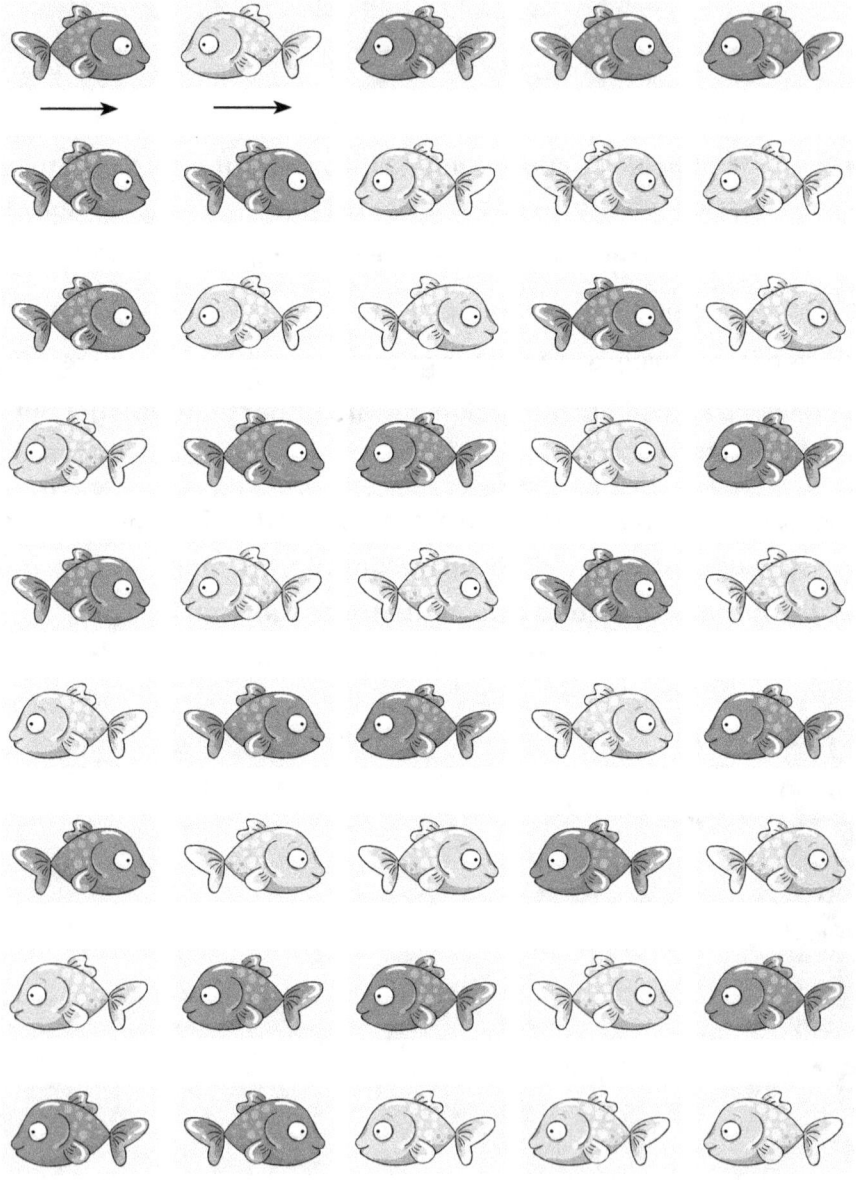

2. What figure should replace the question mark?

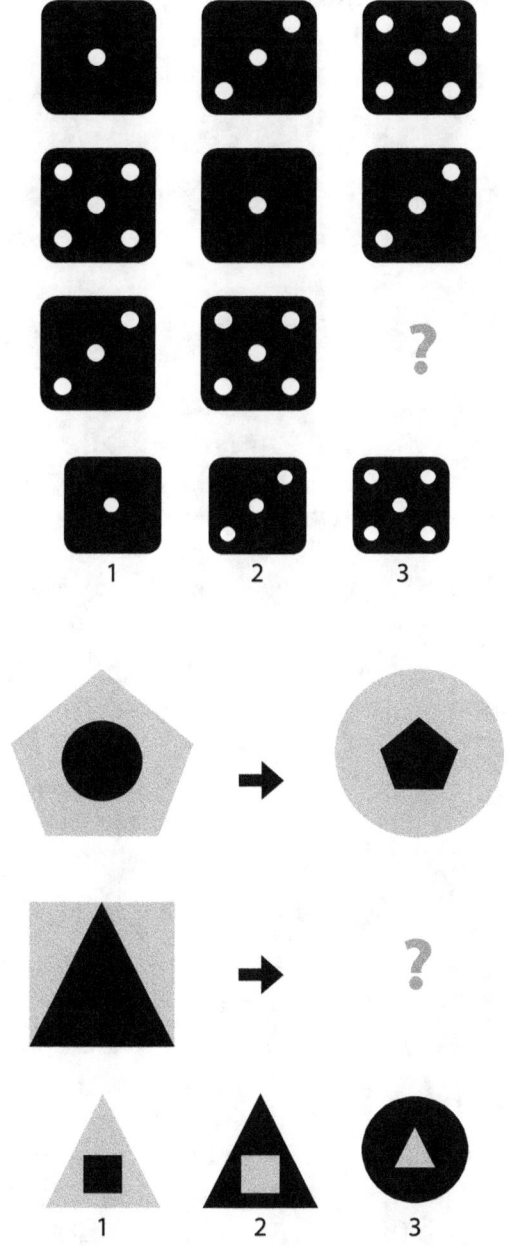

3. Try to say the ink color of the words below as fast as you can, while ignoring the meaning of the word.

Black	White	Black	Gray	White
White	Gray	Black	Black	Gray
White	Black	White	White	Black
Black	White	Gray	Black	Gray
White	Gray	Black	Gray	White
Gray	Gray	White	White	Black
White	Black	Black	Gray	Gray
Black	Gray	White	Black	White
Gray	White	Gray	White	Black
White	Gray	White	Black	Gray
Black	White	Black	Gray	Black

4. Consider the different lines of colorful cards below. Try to cross the cards with the targeted color as it has been marked with "heart" as quickly as possible. Whenever you see the heart mark again, you should change the target color. Start with the gray color as the target.

➡

Decisions & Control

- **Set Daily Goals:** Set at least one goal every day and strive to achieve it by the end of that day. Small goals such as saving $20 while shopping or walking 1/2 a mile, to start are worthwhile. You can gradually set 7 goals for each week and achieve them.

- **Track Your Money:** Try to monitor your daily money spending, even when it is very low, with writing and calculating on paper. Being a good personal money manager will help you to take over control in other aspects of your life.

- **Practice Patience:** Whenever you feel overwhelmed by impulses and emotions to make a decision or take an action: stop, take a deep breath, and close your eyes. Then starting from 10, count up to 20 slowly.

Identify and describe other recovery activities you may be aware of or already be using you believe are useful.

....
....
....
....
....
....
....
....

5. Try to draw a middle circle (between the inside and outside circles) as slowly as you can. Try not to hit the other two circles.

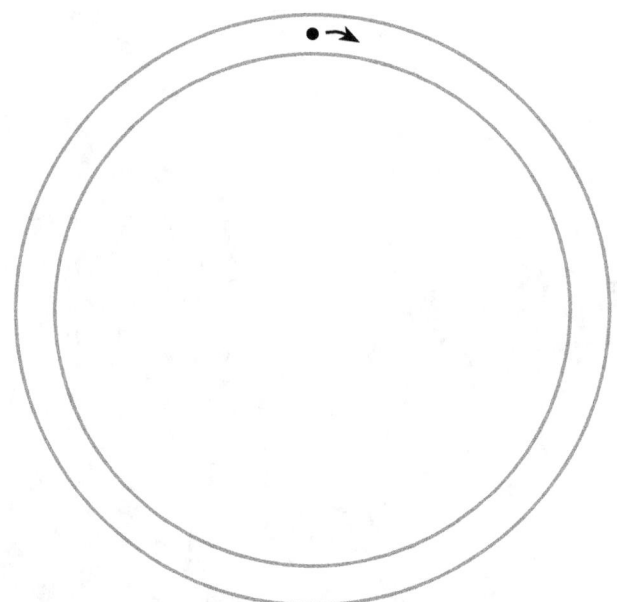

Movement & Speech

I often find myself searching for the right words in conversations, words I used to know in the context for which I seek them. I feel very limited in my vocabulary resources; very unlike I used to feel in conversation which was confident and adept. I find myself stuttering and/or groping for words.

I also feel like my coordination and dexterity have diminished a great deal. Movements and tasks that used to come very easily for me are much more difficult and I feel sluggish. My driving skills and confidence behind the wheel have diminished and this makes me very fearful of being at high-risk to have an accident.

What are the other aspects of "Movement & Speech Deficits" you've experienced in your life? List and discuss them in writing here:

Try to write about the effects of social media on real life communications in one paragraph. You have 5 minutes.

6. Try to find your way from the gray to the black arrow in the below maze as fast as you can.

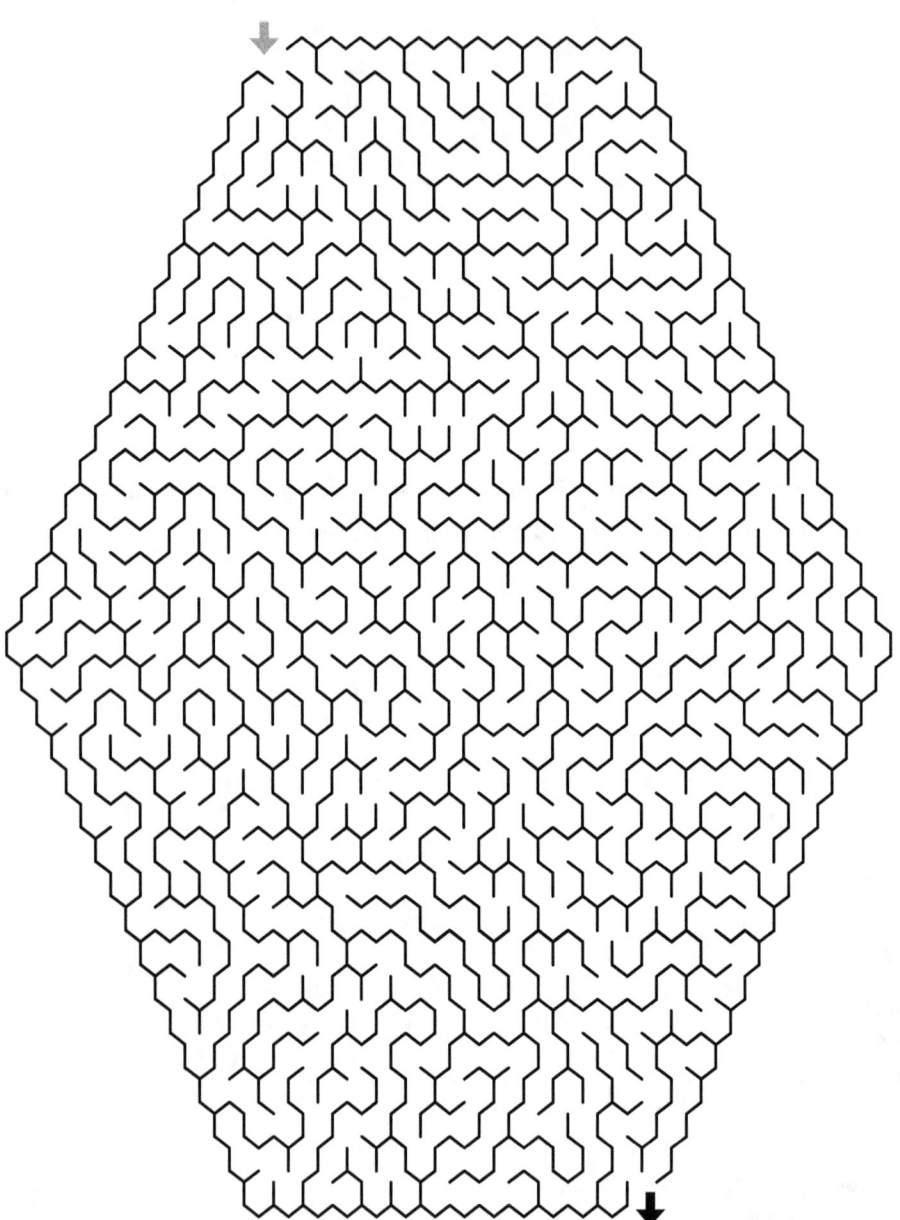

7. Try to draw a line from the black circle to the gray square. But note that you are not allowed to pick up your pencil and shouldn't touch the walls. Your line should be as straight as possible.

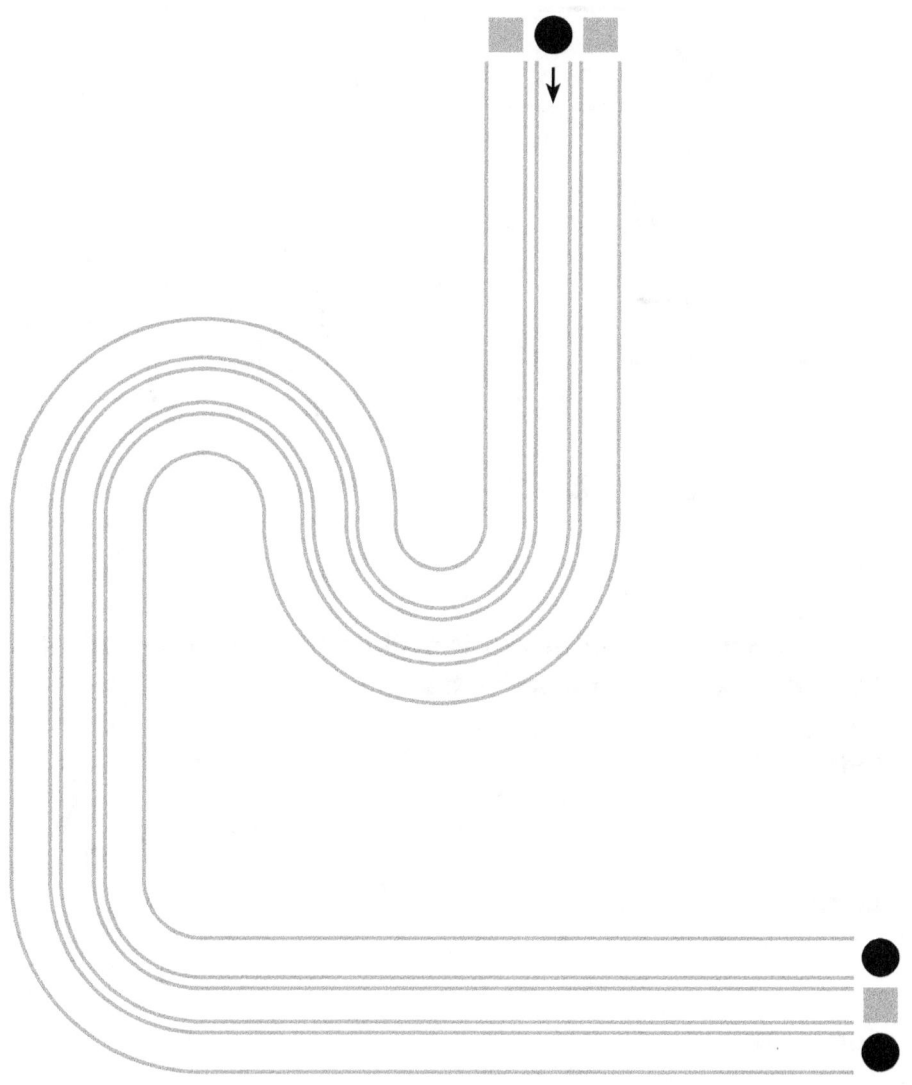

8. Draw the remaining mirrored half of the shape below.

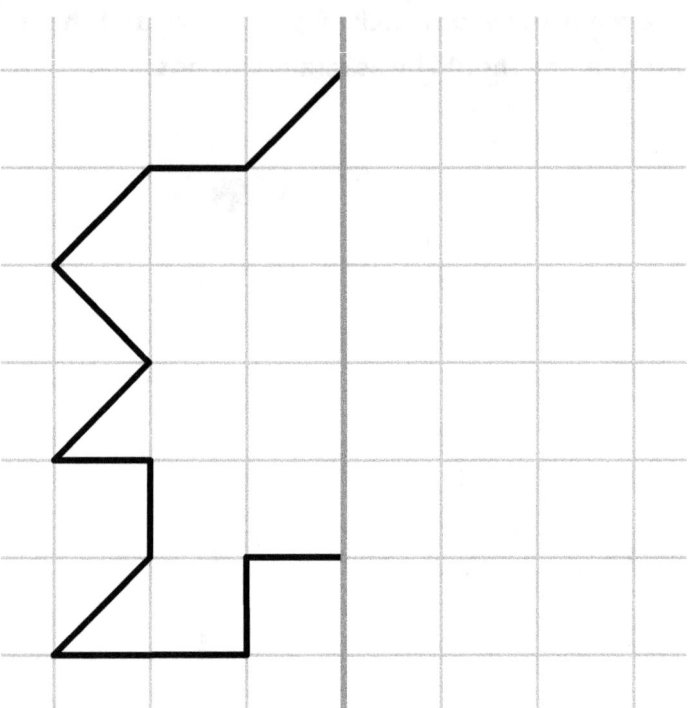

9. Try to write as many as words begin with the determined letter. You have one minute for each letter.

Letter "L":

Letter "A":

Letter "M":

10. Try to trace in between the two sets of line as quickly as you can and without picking up your pencil.

> Practice

Movement & Speech

- **Practice Paraphrasing:** Select a paragraph from recovery literature, a magazine or a newspaper and read it mindfully. Then rewrite the paragraph in your own words, using synonyms and alternative descriptions.

- **Enjoy the "Artist in You":** Grab a coloring book and allow yourself to get colorfully creative! Try to color without going outside the confines of the patterns.

- **Improve Dexterity:** Don Henley, famed drummer for the Eagles, said he first began drumming by tapping on his school books and desk. Sit and intentionally strike drum beats, varied and different paced to improve and stimulate manual dexterity. Enjoy little competitions with yourself around speed, patterns and precision.

Identify and describe other recovery activities you may be aware of or already be using you believe are useful.

....

....

....

11. The picture below is a mobile phone keypad. Try to tap on number 56 with your left index finger for 50 times. Do it as fast as you can.

You can do this exercise using other fingers on your right or left hand. You can change the numbers as well.

Few Suggestions
Commit to abstinence from intoxicants

■ **Avoid** places where you used/drank. Any drug-related cue can activate processes in your brain that are harmful for its health.

■ **Break** relationships with all using partners. Your brain needs new healthy friends to be able to recover.

■ **Affirm** commitment to "total abstinence" from any drug, including alcohol, legal or illegal. Your brain is very vulnerable to any intoxicant during recovery. Take care of it responsibly.

Make a list of 5 behaviors that you would like to change.

....
....
....
....
....

12. Now, to make these changes, you need to use some strategies. See the example below and make your own list.

For example, If you want to reduce the time spent on the internet, You can turn off your cellular data. Or put your phone in a place where you can not easily see it. Or you can close your personal accounts on social media.

....
....
....
....
....
....
....
....
....
....
....

Few Suggestions

Be more physically active

- **Try** to make time for regular exercise and other physical activities. Your brain and body generate chemicals during rigorous physical activity, including workouts that promote your brain recovery.

- **Engage** in aerobic exercises, as recommended for someone of your age, medical condition, build, and gender to promote holistic health but, avoid too much or too intensive exercise.

- **Try** exercising in group-settings for support, encouragement and meet the social needs of your healing brain.

Identify and describe other recovery activities you may be aware of or already be using you believe are useful.

....
....
....
....
....
....
....

You have done the third session and learned about "Control and Decision making" and "Movement and Speech". Now, mark the scales below:

Your mood:

0   1   2   3   4   5   6   7   8   9   10

Level of Achievement:

0   1   2   3   4   5   6   7   8   9   10

Date: .... Time: .... Duration: ....

Number of incorrect answers: ....

Main weak points: ....
....
....

Conclusion: ....
....
....

Part IV

Be more social and feel better

Have you ever experienced difficulties about knowing your weaknesses and abilities and can not find a precise answer to this question that "How can you describe yourself?". Have you found yourself feeling that you can not communicate with other people easily and express your emotions or perceive others.
Welcome to fourth part!

| Awareness and Insight | Social Cognition | Feeling Good |

Awareness & Insight

Despite what some of my friends, relatives, and co-workers might say, I do not see myself as someone who has a disease, needs medical care or other treatment. I only drink and use recreationally and can stop anytime I want to. I simply don't want to. I am tempted to use because it feels good when I use. I like the effects produced by alcohol and/or other drugs, cannot see, in the using brain state, how they hurt me; therefore, I do not see the benefit of abstaining or asking for help.

What are the other aspects of "Awareness & Insight Deficits" you've experienced in your life? List and discuss them in writing here:

....

....

....

Do you strongly agree / believe:

- Long-term stress can negatively affect your brain functions such as memory and attention? ☐ Yes ☐ No
- Your lifestyle can significantly help your brain during recovery period? ☐ Yes ☐ No
- Our brain possesses an incredible ability to repair its damages happens due to stress, drug, etc. ☐ Yes ☐ No
- Impairment of brain functions can intensify negative emotions (such as depression, stress) or addictive behaviors (problematic use of mobile)? ☐ Yes ☐ No
- You can ask for help from a trained coach to support you on track of recovery? ☐ Yes ☐ No

The questions above are some important facts about cognitive rehabilitation. So, the more "No" responses, the more you need to know about this field of therapeutic intervention.

....

....

....

1. Can you describe yourself clearly? You should write about different aspects of your appearance, personality, interests, weak points and everything you say when you introduce yourself to others.

Name one of your partners/friends/colleagues/family members and write down what he/she will answer this question about you and compare with yours

2. Read through the list of adjectives, and circle the eight that you think are the most descriptive of you at present.

Happy	Brave	Emotional
Forgetful	Anxious	Stable
Helpless	Sensitive	Inactive
Calm	Hopeful	Childish
Talkative	Kind	Irritable
Cautious	Reliable	Confident
Changeable	Enthusiastic	Angry
Dependent	Sociable	Withdrawn

How do you rate your insight about your personal characteristics, weaknesses and strength?:

0   1   2   3   4   5   6   7   8   9   10

Not at all   **completely confident**

Awareness & Insight

- **Observe Your Brain Processes:** You can monitor what is happening inside your brain and ask yourself such questions as" "What type of process is my brain engaged in right now?" "What brain processes encourage me to feel certain emotions such as glad, sad, or mad?"

- **Attend to Your Posture:** Use your brain power to monitor your posture moment by moment especially when you are in the middle of walking, typing or watching TV.

- **Live Weight-Conscious:** If your body weight has been a health risk for you, find out what your ideal BMI is. Find brain processes that help you reach your food intake and body weight goals.

Try to imagine three ideal aspects of your life (physical, social, psychological aspects) and then write down about what would happen if they are achieved in your life during the next one and ten years. For example, *If I finish my college degree, I can find a job in a year and save money to buy a small house in ten years.*

One year:

....

....

....

....

....

....

....

Ten years:

....

....

....

....

....

....

....

....

....

Social Cognition

I have difficulty identifying and expressing my emotions, clearly and understandably. I realize that I cannot accurately pick-up on cues coming from other people about how they see me or interpret my behavior, so I have lost my ability to empathize. Because I cannot access this type of insight, communicating with my family and others is especially difficult for me. I also seem to be unable to and uninterested in making new friends.

What are the other aspects of "Social Cognition Deficits" you've experienced in your life? List and discuss them in writing here:

....
....
....
....
....
....
....
....
....
....

Let's play "Mirror Game":

To play this game, form 2-players groups. One player is a main person and the other is the imitator. These roles change repeatedly during the game. The game starts with the main person. He/she starts acting to show different emotions. For example, raising the corners of his/her mouth upwards to show happiness. At the same time, the imitator who stands by 50 cm away in front of the main person, try to watch him/her carefully and recognize the emotion. They change their place after 15 minutes.

This game starts with simple action and then can proceed to the complex ones.

3. Look at the people in the pictures below. Can you put yourself in their places and describe what you might be experiencing.

4. Look at the below faces and try to identify the emotion conveyed in each face.

5. Try to describe the image below with writing a paragraph.

6. Write one paragraph about the below image in 4 minutes.

Practice

Social Cognition

- **Use Compassion and Understanding:** In every meeting, place yourself in other people shoes, try to view the world from their perspective and consider their circumstances.

- **Allow Yourself to be Transparent:** Express your thoughts, fears, and emotions to your recovery friends or family members, when safe to do so whenever you feel out-of-sorts or tense. Use a journal or a notebook to write about emotions you experienced that day.

- **Be a Voice Analyzer:** Listen to your partner's expressions and tone of voice deeply during conversations and try to understand by writing about his/her emotions from voice inflections and body language.

Identify and describe other recovery activities you may be aware of or already be using you believe are useful.

....

....

....

How to write emotional daily journal?

Similar to daily journal in which people write about the events happened to them on the day, writing about the various emotions that we may experience during the day would be a helpful exercise to improve our social interactions. This emotional journal help us to analyze our emotions and become more ready for similar conditions in future.

Now, try to write about the emotions you have experience today so far.

....

....

....

....

....

....

....

....

Feeling Good

The seduction of drugs for me is highly rewarding and beckons me, loudly and frequently. The rewarding experience begins with simply thinking about my drug or obtaining it. It induces a kind of pleasure for me that even thinking about them not just seeing, causes this change. The degree of promised reward from my drug profoundly replaces other formerly pleasurable things. I seem to avoid doing things and going places that I used to enjoy. Without using drugs to change the way I feel, I do not seem to have effective skills to entertain myself or possess a basic interest in doing previously enjoyable activities alone.

What are the other aspects of "Feeling Good Deficits" you've experienced in your life? List and discuss them in writing here:

....

....

....

....

Have you ever:

1. Felt in a way that there is no bright side in your life and everything is dark? ☐ Yes ☐ No

2. Found that there is nothing enjoyable anymore, even the activities that you used to like them? ☐ Yes ☐ No

3. Found meaningless that other people enjoy from simple things? ☐ Yes ☐ No

4. Avoided to participate in group events, party or friend gathering? ☐ Yes ☐ No

5. Found that there is no more rewarding activities in the word? Or something that you are encouraged to do it? ☐ Yes ☐ No

The questions above are some examples of situations that you need to boost your good feeling. So, the more "Yes" responses, the more you need to care about this brain function.

....

....

7. What are the most pleasant activities that you enjoy doing them? Let's make a list. These may include simple pleasures, or things you value or find important. Then rate each of them out of 10 (the most) for the pleasure they can make in YOU.

#	Activity	Rate

8. Try to find as many happy faces in the picture below, without using a pen or pencil to make marks. Then write the number.

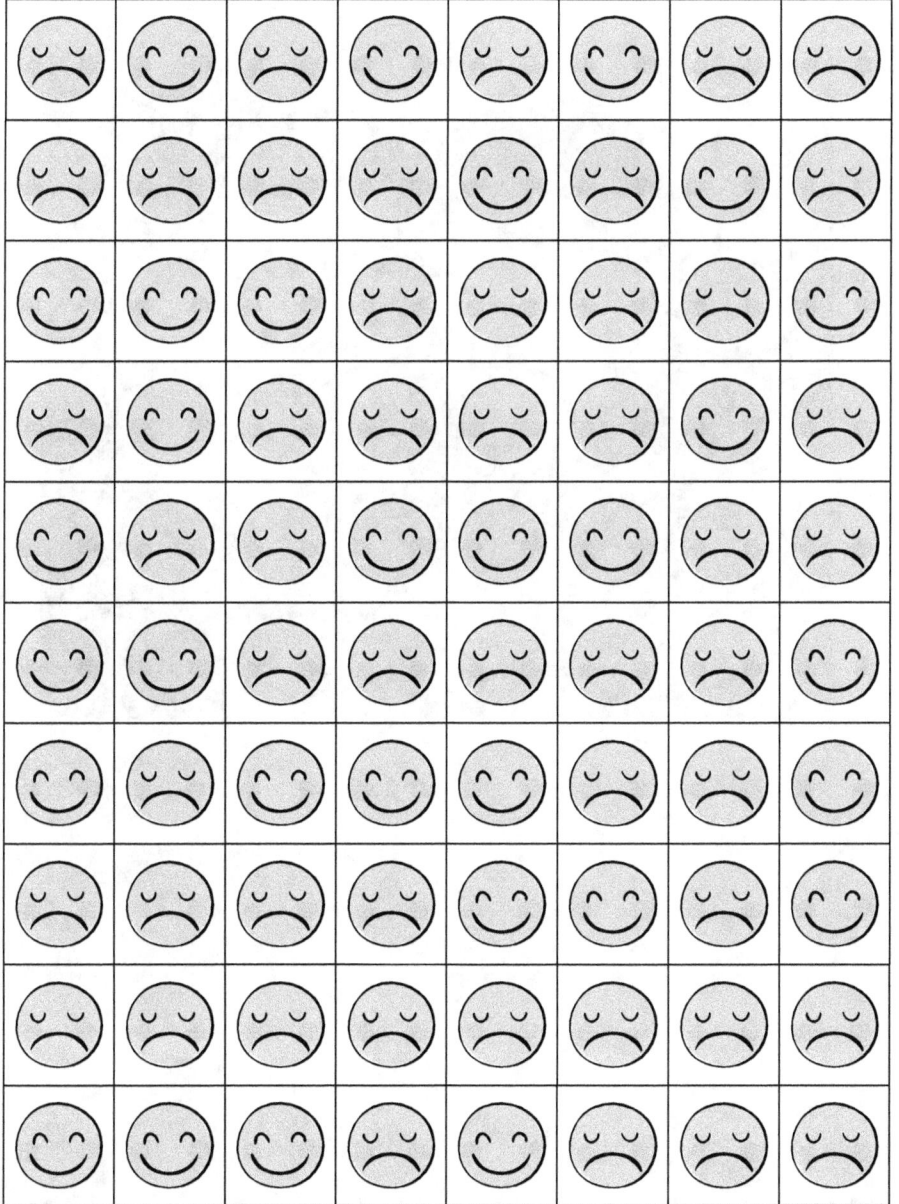

9. Look at the image below and try to write about the positive aspects and the emotions you think the women in the picture might be experiencing.

10. Below, find and count all the positive words as quickly as you can. Then write the number.

Practice
Feeling Good

- **Be a Member of the Happiness Club:** Try to laugh and share humor with other people. Spend your leisure time watching comedy shows with your family and offer some funny stories and tell some jokes. Turn on your sense of humor and enjoy your life.

- **Be a "Hobbiest":** Choose joyful hobbies that help you relax and feel joyful. Ex: Swimming, arts/crafts, cooking, golf or gardening could enhance your recovery and brain healing.

- **Detox Your Brain from Negative Memories by Making New Positive Ones:** Try new fun experiences and form happy memories. You can visit new places or learn new exercises associated with joy and pleasure without using alcohol or any other drugs.

Identify and describe other recovery activities you may be aware of or already be using you believe are useful.

....
....
....
....
....
....
....
....
....
....
....
....
....
....

Try to talk about the words below positively. You have 3 minutes for each word. Try to not use any negative word (such as tiredness, difficult).
1. Sunset
2. Foggy weather
3. Car accident
4. Last day of holidays

Few Suggestions
Be a healthy friend to yourself

- **Be mindful** of your emotions, thoughts and behaviors as often and intentionally as possible.

- **Be willing** to practice yoga or attend any type of meditation classes. Practice meditation exercise as part of a daily program to help your brain progress in recovery.

- **Be willing** to practice mindfulness exercises in daily tasks, such as eating, walking, and cleaning house/yard work, etc. Experiencing normal pleasures from normally pleasurable tasks is a staple of recovery.

Identify and describe other recovery activities you may be aware of or already be using you believe are useful.

....
....
....
....
....
....

When an emotional event happens and we experience different emotions such as happiness, sadness, fear, anger, etc., our senses may perceive these emotions differently. For example when we get angry, our sense of taste may not work well and we can not perceive taste of food, or we may hear some noise like ringing in our ears.

	Anger	Happiness	Anxiety	Sadness
Sight				
Hearing				
Taste				
Smell				
Touch				

Few Suggestions

Be more socially active

- **Get involved** with other people who are living in recovery successfully.

- **Be committed** to engage in 12 step or other mutual support groups regularly.

- **Be willing** to focus on your relationships with people, including family members, who encourage and support your abstinence and recovery.

Identify and describe other recovery activities you may be aware of or already be using you believe are useful.

....
....
....
....
....
....
....

Imagine that you are going to form a social group.

1. What would be the group and the activity you are pursuing to do?

....
....

2. What are your goals?

....
....

3. What are the main criteria for the people who want to be your member?

....
....

4. As a leader, what are the important criteria that you are concerned with them in team work?

....
....

Few Suggestions
Be patient and hopeful

- **Treat** your brain as you would any other injured part of your body that needs extended rest and healing for a period of time to experience recovery.

- **Rely** upon the example of other injuries healing over time, accept that you will achieve your brain health gradually.

- **Gather** with and call upon people in successful recovery to benefit from their experience, strength, and hope.

Identify and describe other recovery activities you may be aware of or already be using you believe are useful. ....

....

Reading motivational books that are motivational and Inspirational are very helpful on the track of recovery. Have you ever read these types of books? Can you name one of them and talk about the key message of the book? ....

....

You have done the forth session and learned about "Awareness and Insight", "Feeling good" and "Social cognition" Now, mark the scales below:

Your mood:

0   1   2   3   4   5   6   7   8   9   10

Level of Achievement:

0   1   2   3   4   5   6   7   8   9   10

Date: .... Time: .... Duration: ....

Number of incorrect answers: ....

Main weak points: ....

....

....

Conclusion: ....

....

....

Concluding Remarks

Recovery from addiction to alcohol and other drugs is a life-long journey. The brain-healing is necessary to restore the damage and regain lost brain functions, also it is vital for sustained addiction recovery. Advances in technology and other research efforts are allowing us to learn more, all the time, about our brain and how we can potentially heal the lost capabilities. Offering yourself continued education about brain health and what that means to assist your progress in recovery, will help you to be better prepared for the challenges that arise on the path of recovery. Testing your brain's resiliency with intentional daily tasks and exercises will offer you more confidence with each successful completion. Use your own creativity and challenge yourself to add different brain exercises to your life in the same way that we have encouraged you to do in the third part of the book. Be daring and imaginative. The more exploratory you are with your brain, the more you will amaze yourself in the journey.

Answers

Part I

1 13

2
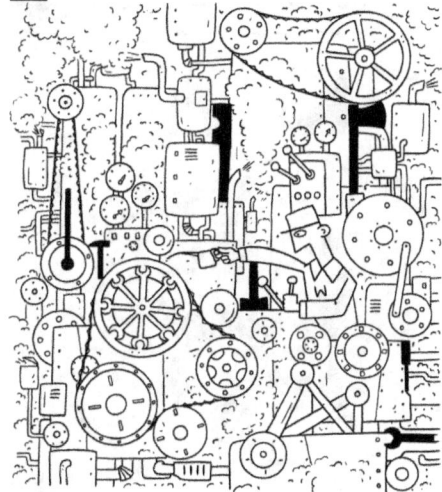

3 6
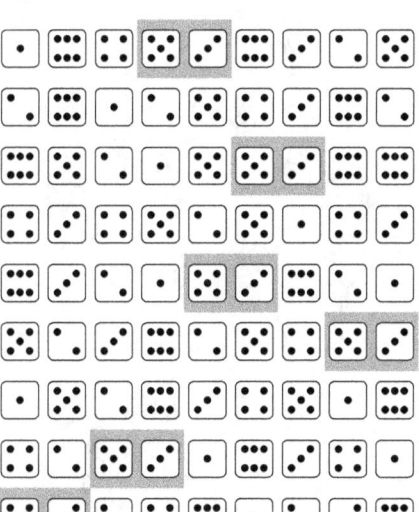

4 BE / BO / SE / BO / BE / BO / BO / SE / BO / BE / SO / BE / SE / BO / SE / BE / BO / BE / SE / BE / BO / BE / BO / BE / SE / SO / BE / BO / BE / BO / BE / SO / BE / SO / BO / BE / SO / BE / BO / BO / SO / BE / BO / BO / SO / BE / BO / SO / BO / SO / BE / SE / BO / SE / BO / SO / SE / BE / BE / BE / SE / BO / SO / BO / SO / SE / BO / SO / BE / BO / BO / SE / BO / BO / BE / SE / SO

7 6

9 A) b. 5 people / B) a. Cat / C) a. Dish / D) c. Tea

11 a. Right / b. Left / c. Left / d. Left / e. Right / f. Left / g. Right / h. Left

Part II

1 Tea / Fork / Kitchen / Table / Bird / Note / Net / Park / Window / Pen / Pizza

6
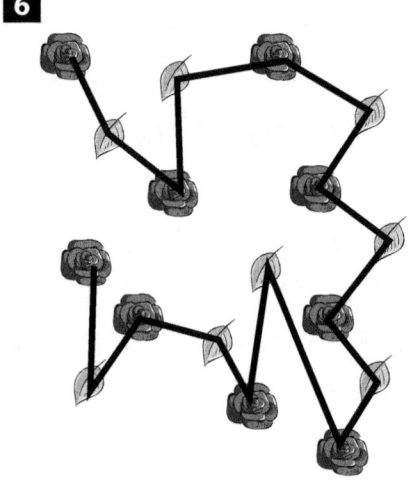

8 9 light blue circles
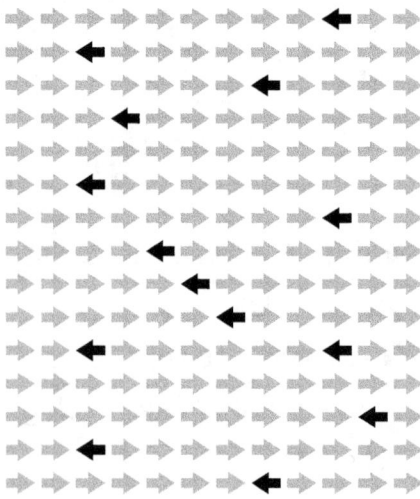

Part III

1
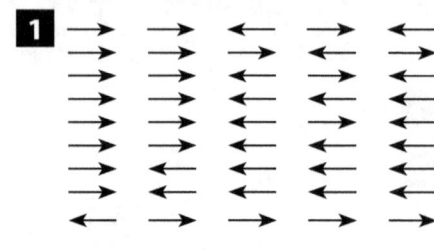

2 3. ⬛ / 2. ▲

4

6
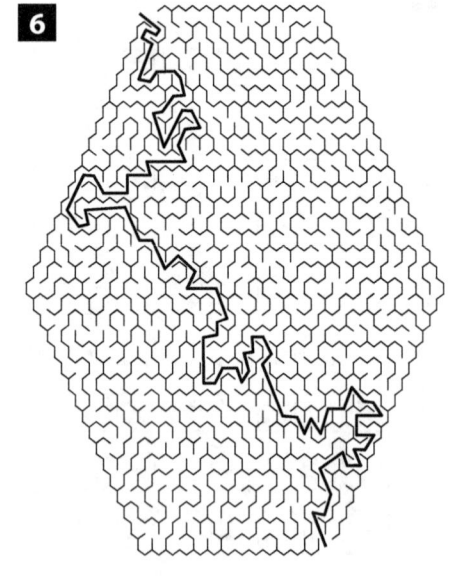

9 L: Lamp / Ladder / Lady / Leaf / Lemon / Lock / Lion / Lizard / Lantern / Lips
A: Apple / Ant / Arrow / Axe / Anchor / Airplane / Arm / Angry / Actor / Angel
M: Moon / Mother / Mouse / Money / Milk / Monkey / Mask / Man / Mug / Muffin

Part IV

4 1. Surprise / 2. Joy / 3. Anger / 4. Anxious / 5. Fear / 6. Suspicious / 7. Satisfied / 8. Annoyed / 9. Angry / 10. Worry / 11. Anticipation / 12. Suspicious / 13. Joy / 14. Sadness / 15. Thoughtful / 16. Disappolntment

8 30 happy faces

10 Good / Kindness / Happy / Joy / Ideal / Up / Great

www.ingramcontent.com/pod-product-compliance
Lightning Source LLC
LaVergne TN
LVHW051526070426
835507LV00023B/3326